STUCK! STRATEGIES

What to Do When Students Get **STUCK**
How to Turn "No!" Into "Let's Go!"

Janice Carroll and Terry Ellis Izraelevitz

Foreword by Christine Hazard, PhD

PUBLISHING

P.O. Box 23173
Shawnee Mission, Kansas 66283-0173
www.aapcpublishing.net

©2015 AAPC Publishing
P.O. Box 23173
Shawnee Mission, Kansas 66283-0173
www.aapcpublishing.net

Publisher's Cataloging-in-Publication

Carroll, Janice (Janice Santogrossi)

STUCK! strategies : what to do when students get STUCK : how to turn "no!" into "let's go!" / Janice Carroll and Terry Ellis Izraelevitz ; foreword by Christine Hazard. -- Shawnee Mission, Kansas : AAPC Publishing, [2015]

pages ; cm.

ISBN: 978-1-937473-99-0
LCCN: 2014952508
Includes bibliographical references.
Summary: Practical and research-based ideas and strategies are presented in two categories, proactive and redirective, to help motivate students with challenging behaviors, including autism spectrum disorders, and ultimately help them succeed. This includes removing "barriers" posed by lack of skills, lack of motivation, sensory issues, and more.--Publisher.

1. Teachers of children with disabilities--Handbooks, manuals, etc. 2. Special education teachers--Handbooks, manuals, etc. 3. Teaching-- Aids and devices. 4. Children with autism spectrum disorders--Education. 5. Autistic children--Education. 6. Asperger's syndrome-- Patients--Education. 7. Children with disabilities--Education. I. Izraelevitz, Terry Ellis. II. Title. III. Title: STUCK strategies.

LC4717 .C37 2015
371.94--dc23   1410

Art: Cover art ©Shutterstock.com

Picture symbols in the visual schedules made using Boardmaker®; www.mayer-johnson.com

This book is designed in Ad Lib and Myriad Pro.

Printed in the United States of America.

Contents

Foreword

Ten years ago, I began a professional relationship with two colleagues in the Los Alamos Public Schools, Janice Carroll and Terry Izraelevitz. Both excellent practitioners, they shared generously of their expertise with me, and several years later our collaboration morphed into the school district's Autism Spectrum Disorders Resource Team, which continues today.

Over the years, Janice and Terry spent several summers together serving students in an ESY (extended school year) program. After one such summer session, they shared something exciting with me. They had put together some ideas that they found significantly helped them in their work with challenging children. They called the ideas STUCK Strategies. Why "stuck"?, I asked. Janice explained that as she and her husband struggled to support their temperamentally difficult first child, they learned that "stuck" is a helpful way to think of children with sensory integration issues. Terry's skills at moving students through challenging behavior echoed this idea – she helped them get unstuck! In the years since, the term "stuck" and the strategies turned out to be meaningful to other parents, teachers, therapists, and administrators. This book now shares the strategies with a larger audience.

The STUCK Strategies are more than a catchy name. They are method based and user friendly, and they incorporate both the science and the art of good practice. Behavioral science tells us that the best intervention is prevention. Antecedent-based management interventions help prevent behavior problems. You will note that the STUCK Strategies are primarily antecedent-based and are designed to precede escalating behavior. Ross Greene, author of *The Explosive Child* and *Lost at School,* writes that "our explanation guides our intervention." Thus, the way we explain behavior to ourselves is critical in deciding on a course of action with a challenging student. Explaining difficult behavior as "stuck" behavior helps us focus on getting the student "unstuck" rather than on distracting variables like stubbornness, opposition, etc. Dr. Greene also points out that children do well when they can. To do that, in many cases, they need support and education (proactive interventions), not punishment and consequences (reactive). Certainly, what I have observed in classrooms from preschool to high school confirms the truth of this statement: Children are happier, safer, and make more progress when staff think proactively. Every teacher and therapist working with behaviorally challenged children needs an arsenal of tools, the primary one being a plan! The strategies detailed in this book will help you notice problems early on and intervene preventively.

As a team, we have come to think of STUCK behavior on a spectrum, from relatively benign to extreme. You will notice in the strategies in this book that the authors have tried to give an example from each end of that spectrum. The examples of specific behaviors and suggested strategies are clearly not exhaustive. In that sense, you will find few details but lots of repetition of important principles. The art of behavioral intervention lies in the way a strategy is implemented by an individual practitioner. You will undoubtedly find that some of the strategies make more sense to you than others, and when using them you will develop personal variations in the way you apply the principles involved. Try them all and see what works for you!

Christine Hazard, PhD

The Origin of "STUCK"

In 1992 I gave birth to our first daughter. During her first day on the planet, her pediatrician noted that our daughter liked to be held. Little did we know that this simple observation was a foreshadowing of many sleepless nights and stressful days to come.

During the first months and years of her life, our daughter actively resisted sleep, demanded frequent feedings, and cried during activities we expected her to enjoy such as walks in her stroller. One of her first words was "ut," which became "tut," and later, "tuk." As a speech-language pathologist, I was fascinated by my daughter's speech sound development. At some point, even before she achieved completely correct articulation of the word, I realized she was saying, "STUCK."

Exhausted and worried, we sought help. One therapist suggested we read the book *SenseAbilities* by Maryann Trott and her colleagues. On page 5, they write that one of the first words used by children with sensory integration issues is "stuck" or similar terms that describe difficult or unpleasant situations (Trott, Laurel, & Windeck, 1993).

Fast-forward a decade. During the summer of 2007, I watched as my co-author worked with a challenging student and brought him – through repeated refusals – to having a successful session. Later, in complimenting her on her skills, I said, "We should write these strategies down." So we did! Thus, we compiled the STUCK Strategies.

In the years since, the term "stuck" and the strategies we used to help students get "unstuck" resonated with parents, teachers, therapists, and administrators. Instructional assistants told us, "Finally, something we can use with our students tomorrow." Our assistant superintendent praised our work saying, "I love the word 'stuck' because we all get stuck sometimes." Indeed we do, and here are some suggestions for helping you get your students "unstuck."

Janice Carroll

Introduction

This book is a collection of strategies we have learned across decades from various sources, including experts and other professionals, as well as students from preschool children to adults with disabilities such as autism spectrum disorders (ASD), communication disorders, developmental delays, Down Syndrome, and inflexible temperament. We have applied the strategies in school, home, and community environments with across-the-board success.

Our bottom line is that "Children [students] do well if they can" (Greene, 2005), and we see it as our job as professionals and parents to make sure they can! We hope you will find the strategies helpful to you and your STUCK students.

STUCK Strategies are ...

▶ *Proactive.* By creating teaching situations that cause student engagement to happen rather than responding to problem behavior after it happens, the adult is in control and the student learns. You must have a plan!

▶ *Positive.* STUCK Strategies prevent challenging behaviors from occurring, support the learning of new skills, and ensure problem behaviors are not effective.

▶ *Supportive.* When a student gets STUCK, ask yourself, "What kind of support does this student need?" rather than "Why is this student trying to ruin my day?" As Nathan Ory, Canadian psychologist, says, "When you see confusion, offer a peaceful, helpful hand." We say, "Offer a STUCK Strategy."

▶ *Preventive.* The best way to avoid reinforcing problem behavior – that is, causing it to occur more frequently in the future – is to **prevent** the behavior from occurring in the first place. STUCK Strategies are part of an antecedent management approach to teaching, which means that we focus on interventions that change student behavior by manipulating conditions that precede their behavior, for example, room arrangement and choice of activities.

▶ *Effective.* We use STUCK Strategies on a daily basis in our work with students of various ages and disabilities. STUCK Strategies are tried and true. We **know** they work!

Students get **STUCK** because they ...

⁝ *Have a knee-jerk reaction to say "No!"* Many of our students have temperaments wired to go reflexively to refusal when presented with teaching tasks (Greene, 2005).

⁝ *Lack skills.* Many of our students lack the skills (language, academic, motor, sensory regulation) to do the tasks adults present in teaching situations.

⁝ *Don't know how to start.* Many of our students do not know how to begin tasks in teaching situations.

⁝ *Have limited task persistence.* Many of our students have experienced frequent failure in teaching situations and are not capable of staying the course through to completion.

⁝ *Have low frustration tolerance.* Many of our students cannot deal with teaching situations because of their distorted views of the difficulty and their ability to cope.

⁝ *Don't see the point.* Many of our students do not share our perspective about the teaching process. Many adults expect their agenda to be their students' agenda. The "art" of teaching is making your agenda the students' agenda. Teachers who design activities that are ability-appropriate, meaningful, functional, of appropriate length, and supportive, are masters of this art.

⁝ *Create a "neural rut."* Many of our students use refusal behavior so frequently (and effectively) in teaching situations that getting STUCK becomes their most practiced, most likely, neural path.

What **STUCK** looks like . . .

⁝ Obvious: "No"

No response

Stopping in the middle of a task

Attempts to leave the teaching situation

Agitation

Falling to the floor

Meltdowns

"I can't"

"I don't know"

▶ Less obvious: Poor attention

                                  Stalling

                                  Off-task comments/behaviors

                                  Skipping steps in a sequence

                                  Slow responding

                                  Puzzled facial expression (confusion)

                                  Perseverative/repetitive behaviors

                                  Increased activity level (e.g., wiggling in the chair)

How the Book Is Organized

We organized the material for this book into 15 distinct strategies in two categories: proactive STUCK Strategies and redirective STUCK Strategies. While not a hard-and-fast rule, we recommend, at least initially, that you try the strategies in the order presented here. You will develop favorites and learn which strategies work best for you and your students. Not all STUCK Strategies will work every time in every situation.

Our description of each strategy includes instructions for implementation under the headings: BASICS, MATERIALS, EXAMPLES OF USING THIS STRATEGY TO SUPPORT STUDENTS IN MOVING AWAY FROM STUCK BEHAVIOR, and REFERENCES. In addition, we provide illustrations as visual supports for better and easier comprehension.

Finally, the appendices contain the principles that guide our work with students, the STUCK Strategies on one page for easy reference, and a STUCK Strategies worksheet for planning.

JSC & TEI

Terminology

We use the term "adult" to mean any teacher, therapist, instructional assistant, parent, or caregiver working with a "student." We use the term "student" to mean any-age learner in a teaching situation. Finally, we alternate use of the pronouns "he" and "she."

PROACTIVE STUCK STRATEGIES

1. STRATEGY: DEVELOPMENTALLY APPROPRIATE & MEANINGFUL ACTIVITIES

> *We purposefully made this the first strategy because this is where we start when planning behavior interventions for our students who get stuck. Failure to teach meaningful and developmentally appropriate material is the cause of much STUCK behavior. If this strategy is not correctly in place, none of the other strategies will work. No amount of support will enable a preschooler to do calculus!*

THE BASICS:

✔ Know your student's cognitive, language, motor, behavioral, and sensory levels, as determined through standardized testing, observation, and consultation with team members.

✔ Consult your student's teachers, speech-language pathologist (SLP), occupational therapist (OT), physical therapist (PT), and school psychologist through team meetings, email, and communication notebooks.

✔ Determine your student's interests, preferences, and dislikes through observation, student interview, preference surveys, and consultation with parents and previous teachers.

✔ Remember instructional time is limited!

✔ Bear in mind that students need to learn skills they will use in multiple environments, such as home, school, work, and the community.

✔ Include instruction of skills that are relevant and functional and that make a difference in the student's life (e.g., toileting, dressing, interacting socially, managing a personal schedule).

✔ Ask yourself, "*Why* am I doing *this* activity with *this* student at *this* time?"

✔ Spend time planning instructional methods, materials, and behavioral supports.

EXAMPLES OF USING THE STRATEGY TO SUPPORT STUDENTS IN MOVING AWAY FROM STUCK BEHAVIOR

STUCK Behavior: Student does not sing the "days of the week" song.

Adult: Switches to teaching more relevant and functional skills such as the days of the week as they relate to the student's personal schedule – which days are work days, which days are school days, and which days are home days.

STUCK Behavior: Student tears his math paper in two.

Adult: Fine-tunes the lesson to the student's ability level.

REFERENCES:

Janzen, J. E. (2003). *Understanding the nature of autism: A guide to autism spectrum disorders* (2nd ed.). San Antonio, TX: Harcourt Assessment.

Partington, J. (2010). *The assessment of basic language and learning skills – revised* (Vol. 3). Pleasant Hill, CA: Behavior Analysts.

Rogers, S. J., & Dawson, G. (2010). *Early start Denver Model for young children with autism: Promoting language, learning, and engagement.* New York, NY: Guilford Press.

2. STRATEGY: CLEARLY COMMUNICATE EXPECTATIONS

THE BASICS:

✔ Plan what you want the student to do.

✔ Tell the student explicitly what you expect.

✔ Present expectations verbally *and* visually.

✔ Remember that the "art" of teaching is making *your* agenda the student's agenda.

✔ Give instructions, then wait expectantly.

✔ Use body language, tone of voice, and proximity that communicate your expectations for compliance and your availability for support.

MATERIALS:

• Visual schedules, such as the following, are examples of visual representations of expectations:

Deskwork	✓
Animal Video	✓
Deskwork	✓
Computers	

Working from top to bottom, the student makes a check in the box after completing each task.

• Cards such as the following are visual representations of behavioral expectations.

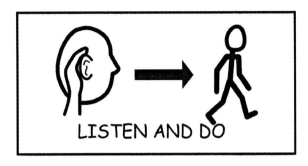

Before beginning an activity, the adult reviews behavioral expectation cards with the student. Then, instead of stopping an activity to verbally remind or redirect the student, the adult shows or points to the appropriate behavioral expectation card.

EXAMPLES OF USING THIS STRATEGY TO SUPPORT STUDENTS IN MOVING AWAY FROM STUCK BEHAVIOR

STUCK Behavior: Student asks, "Are we done yet?"

Adult: Presents a mini-schedule as a concrete way to represent the sequence of tasks remaining.

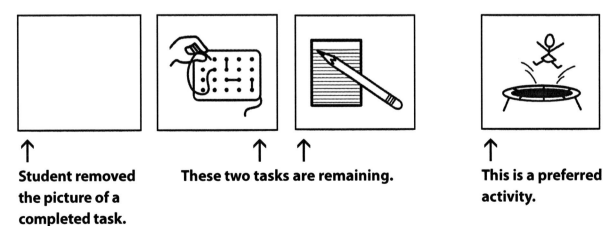

Student removed the picture of a completed task.   **These two tasks are remaining.**   **This is a preferred activity.**

STUCK Behavior: Student yells "no" when adult presents materials.

Adult: Arranges materials in trays or on shelves, with work to be done on the student's left and finished work on the student's right and a surface (desk or table) for the student to work in the middle (e.g., TEACCH workstation).

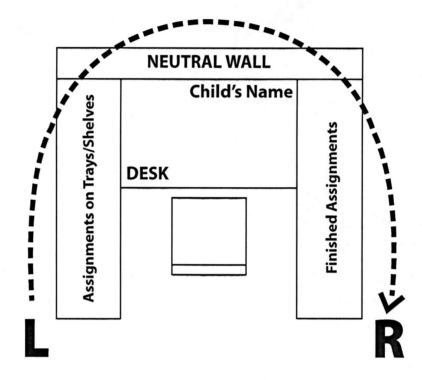

TEACCH workstation conceptual diagram (Henriksen & Kaup, 2009).

REFERENCES:

Henriksen, K., & Kaup, M. L. (2009). Supportive learning environments for children with autism spectrum disorders. *Undergraduate Research Journal for the Human Sciences, 9.* Retrieved from http://www.kon.org/urc/urc_research_journal9.html

Janzen, J. E. (2003). *Understanding the nature of autism: A guide to autism spectrum disorders* (2nd ed.). San Antonio, TX: Harcourt Assessment.

Schopler, E., Mesibov, G., & Hearsey, K. (1995). Structured teaching in the TEACCH system. In E. Schopler & G. Mesibov (Eds.), *Learning and cognition in autism* (pp. 243-268). New York: NY Plenum Press.

3. STRATEGY: VISUAL SCHEDULE AND "FINISHED, NOW, NEXT"

THE BASICS:

✔ Look to your SLP or other staff member who is knowledgeable about visual supports to orchestrate the design of the student's visual schedule. Visual schedules can be as simple as a handwritten checklist and as complex as an individualized picture system. See references below for details on designing visual schedules.

✔ Keep in mind that visual supports are *receptive* language supports that augment the adult's verbalizations.

✔ Address the student's need for predictability.

✔ Represent the variety, amount, and sequence of activities on the visual schedule (see Illustration a.).

✔ Provide a concrete way to track students' progress toward completion of their work on the visual schedule (see Illustration b.).

✔ Focus on three-activity segments of the day's schedule (see Illustration c.).

✔ Plan the order of activities to balance the student's needs, attention span, sensory differences, likes, dislikes, and familiarity with activities (Janzen, 2003).

✔ Consider outdoor vs. indoor, passive vs. active, and student-directed vs. adult-directed activities.

✔ Use priming = "readying the student to be ready" (Ory, 2007).

✔ Remove schedule cards from the student's visual schedule or check tasks off a list to reinforce completion of activities (see Illustration c.).

MATERIALS:

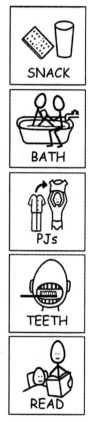

- Digital camera and/or Boardmaker®
  (www.mayer-johnson.com/boardmaker) to create
  photos or symbols for making visual schedules

- Cardstock paper

- Laminating film or clear Contact® paper

- Hook-and-loop fasteners

- File folders, ring binders, etc., to hold the schedule

a. These visual schedules illustrate the variety, amount, and sequence
   of activities in completing work to get to a preferred activity and
   preparing for bed – that is, reading and time on the computer,
   respectively.

b. The visual schedule here is a checklist of the
   steps required to complete a worksheet.
   When the adult assigns a worksheet, the
   student refers to the checklist and checks
   off each item as completed. The checklist
   may be attached to the worksheet, inserted
   in the student's binder, or placed on the
   student's desk.

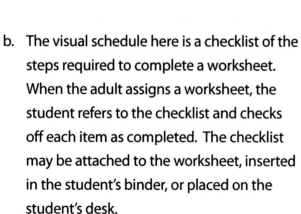

c. This is an example of the visual schedule of a preschool student with ASD. Each card, affixed to the page with hook-and-loop fasteners, represents an activity in the student's day. As the student finishes an activity, she may remove the card depicting that activity and place the card in a pocket labeled "finished" as the adult says, "Motor is FINISHED. NOW it is time for Group. NEXT you will go Outside. Let's go to Group."

EXAMPLES OF USING THE STRATEGY TO SUPPORT STUDENTS IN MOVING AWAY FROM STUCK BEHAVIOR

STUCK Behavior: Student pushes materials off the table.

Adult: Shows the student his schedule and says, "It's time for math NOW. NEXT, you will have computer time. Let's do math."

STUCK Behavior: Student heads for the playroom when told to get ready for bed.

Adult: Points to the student's visual schedule (see illustration a.) and says, "You're FINISHED with your snack. NOW it is time for your bath. NEXT, we will put on your favorite PJs. Let's go take that bath NOW!"

REFERENCES:

Janzen, J. E. (2003). *Understanding the nature of autism: A guide to autism spectrum disorders* (2nd ed.). San Antonio, TX: Harcourt Assessment.

Ory, N. (2007). *Working with people with challenging behaviors: A guide for maintaining positive relationships*. New Lennox, IL: High Tide Press.

Savner, J. L., & Myles, B. S. (2000). *Making visual supports work in the home and community*. Shawnee Mission, KS: AAPC Publishing.

4. STRATEGY: SENSORY BREAK

THE BASICS:

✔ Contact your OT to assess the student's sensory needs and develop appropriate sensory strategies.

✔ Understand that sensory input influences behavioral output (e.g., a student jumps on a trampoline and then is ready to return to complete deskwork).

✔ Remember that sensory systems include seeing, hearing, smelling, touching, tasting, moving the head (vestibular), and moving the body (proprioceptive).

✔ Include sensory breaks in the student's daily schedule as positive support for the student.

✔ Think of sensory breaks as opportunities for the student to *move* the whole body, put something in the *hands,* or put something in the *mouth* in order to calm, alert, or organize for the task at hand.

✔ Note that, as a rule of thumb, moving with resistance such as carrying a stack of books to the library, squeezing a ball, chewing gum, or sucking hard candy is calming, alerting, and organizing to the central nervous system, thus readying the student to move away from being STUCK.

✔ Individualize breaks according to the student's sensory needs and preferences in consultation with your OT.

✔ Use sensory breaks as prevention strategies *before* problem behaviors occur rather than as consequences for problem behaviors.

✔ Note that the adult, not the student, sets the rules around the use of sensory breaks (e.g., the number of push-ups, how long the student is out of the room, the gum stays in the student's mouth).

MATERIALS:

Possible choices, depending on the student's needs and the environment, include the following:

Move: The Whole Body

- mini-trampoline

- stretch bands

- play structure

- weighted balls

- stack of heavy books or weighted box/backpack

- inflatable seat cushion   (e.g., www.gymnic.com)

- large inflatable ball

Move: Hands

- fidget toy

- prop for a given activity (e.g., an object related to the book being read at Circle)

- puppets

Move: Mouth

- water bottle

- fruit chews

- pretzels

EXAMPLES OF USING THE STRATEGY TO SUPPORT STUDENTS IN MOVING AWAY FROM STUCK BEHAVIOR

STUCK Behavior: Preschool student has a history of leaving Circle.

Adult: Directs the student to sit in cube chair with a moving cushion at the *beginning* of Circle.

STUCK Behavior: Preschool student attempts to leave Circle.

Adult: Hands the student an object to hold. (May be a preferred toy the student has access to *only* at Circle.)

STUCK Behavior: Elementary-age student moves in his seat, which is *beginning* to distract classmates.

Adult:

1. Signals (discreetly) the student to do chair push-ups, OR

2. Tells student to deliver a weighted box to the school office, OR

3. Directs the entire class to stand and stretch, OR

4. Offers the student a water bottle or a stick of gum.

STUCK Behavior: Student bites her hand.

Adult: Approaches the student, handing her a water bottle with a straw, then walks with the student out of the classroom. (We assume the classroom in this example is staffed by more than one adult.) The student and adult return to the classroom after walking for a predetermined amount of time.

REFERENCES:

Fisher, A. G., Murray, E. A., & Bundy, A. C. (1991). *Sensory integration: Theory and practice*. Philadelphia, PA: F. A. Davis Company.

Williams, M. S., & Shellenberg, S. (1996). *How does your engine run?: A leader's guide to the alert program for self-regulation*. Albuquerque, NM: Therapy Works.

5. STRATEGY: CHOICES

THE BASICS:

✔ Allow the student to have a sense of control, which is likely to motivate the student to participate and remain engaged longer.

✔ Offer choices within the ongoing activity (meal, chore, lesson).

✔ Include choices of materials, people, sequence of tasks.

✔ Honor the student's choice.

✔ Help the student get to "yes" (i.e., come around to participating) by giving him some control of the situation.

✔ Realize choice can be very powerful but requires quick thinking to determine appropriate choices at the moment needed.

MATERIALS:

• Developmentally appropriate materials and activities

• Circular choice board (see page 22)

EXAMPLES OF USING THE STRATEGY TO SUPPORT STUDENTS IN MOVING AWAY FROM STUCK BEHAVIOR

STUCK Behavior: Student does not respond to the direction, "Clean up your room."

Adult: Asks, "Do you want to put toys in the basket or books on the shelf?" The adult performs the task the student did not choose and continues to offer choices until the room is clean.

STUCK Behavior: Student does not sit at Circle.

Adult: Asks, "Do you want to sit on a stool or a cube chair at Circle?"

STUCK Behavior: Student asks, "How much more 'til I'm done?"

Adult: Responds, "We are going to do two more math pages. Which one do you want to do first?"

STUCK Behavior: Student drops to the floor when told to walk to the bus.

Adult: Asks, "Do you want to walk with Mrs. C. or Mrs. I.?"

STUCK Behavior: Student yells and runs away when offered an activity reinforcer (e.g., a turn in the ball pit).

Adult: Offers a choice board (see below).

CHOICE BOARD

Attaching choice symbols around the circle on the choice board prompts the student to make true choices rather than selecting from left to right.

6. STRATEGY: "COME, DO, START"

THIS AND THE NEXT FOUR STRATEGIES ADDRESS THE NEED FOR PREDICTABILITY AND STRUCTURE, WHICH IS VERY IMPORTANT FOR STUDENTS WITH ASD AND SIMILAR DISABILITIES.

THE BASICS:

✔ Say "COME, DO, START" to calm and focus the student.

✔ Use "COME, DO, START" to support the student in knowing how to get started.

✔ Employ "COME, DO, START" to respond to the student's need for structure by leading the student to what to do next rather than attending to the student's STUCK behavior.

MATERIALS:

• "COME, DO, START" chart on page 25

EXAMPLES OF USING THE STRATEGY TO SUPPORT STUDENTS IN MOVING AWAY FROM STUCK BEHAVIOR

STUCK Behavior: Student does not follow a direction to work at the table.

Adult: Says, "COME to the table. DO the puzzle. START with the truck piece."

STUCK Behavior: Student says, "I can't" and drops to the floor.

Adult: Says, "COME to your desk. DO your math page. START with problem one."

STUCK Behavior: Student does not follow a direction to set the table.

Adult: Says, "COME to the kitchen. DO the table setting. START with the plates."

REFERENCE:

Ory, N. (2007). *Working with people with challenging behaviors: A guide for maintaining positive relationships.* New Lennox, IL: High Tide Press.

COME, DO, START

Copy and post the image on page 25 on a staff bulletin board or in the classroom where it will remind adults to use "COME, DO, START."

NOT

NO
DON'T
STOP

Students REACT to these words.

(Adapted from Ory, 2007)

SAY . . .

COME
DO
START

Students RESPOND to these words.

7. STRATEGY: A PROP, A ROLE, AND A RULE

THE BASICS:

✔ A PROP = an object to hold.

✔ A ROLE = a job to do.

✔ A RULE = a statement of the guidelines for expected behavior.

✔ Props provide a tangible path between where you are and where you are going (a.k.a. a transitional object).

✔ A heavy prop provides sensory input that calms and focuses the student (see STUCK Strategy 4).

✔ Students with ASD and students with inflexible temperament respond to rules.

MATERIALS:

• Assorted props

EXAMPLES OF USING THE STRATEGY TO SUPPORT STUDENTS IN MOVING AWAY FROM STUCK BEHAVIOR

↑
Clipboard with class list attached.

↑
Bus leader badge.

↑
Picture of the bus on the student's visual schedule.

STUCK Behavior: Student does not follow classmates to the bus.

Adult: Uses the PROPS above and states the ROLE of the student and the RULE the student follows.

Prop: "Get your <u>clipboard</u> and <u>badge</u>."

Role: "Be the <u>bus leader</u>."

Rule: "We follow the leader to the bus."

(The student leads the class to the bus, checks off names on the clipboard as classmates get on the bus, and then hands the clipboard to the bus driver.)

| headphones | door holder | fire alarm |

STUCK Behavior: Student covers his ears and freezes when the fire drill alarm rings.

Adult: Uses the PROP above and states the ROLE of the student and the RULE the student follows.

Prop "Get your <u>headphones</u>."

Role "Be the <u>door holder</u>."

Rule "Everyone leaves the building when the fire alarm rings."

REFERENCE:

Ory, N. (2007). *Working with people with challenging behaviors: A guide for maintaining positive relationships.* New Lennox, IL: High Tide Press.

REDIRECTIVE STUCK
STRATEGIES

8. STRATEGY: VISUAL REPRESENTATION OF TIME

THE BASICS:

✔ Bear in mind that passage of time and duration of an activity are abstract concepts often not understood by students with special needs.

✔ Use a Time Timer® or similar tool to provide visual representation of the time and duration of an activity.

✔ Use this strategy when a student gets STUCK in the middle of an activity or when a student does not finish or does not stop an activity.

✔ Enforce the rule that only adults set the timer.

MATERIALS:

● Time Timer® (wristwatch, 3", 8", 12", computer screen) (www.timetimer.com)

● Sand timer

● Clock

● Time Tracker®

EXAMPLES OF USING THE STRATEGY TO SUPPORT STUDENTS IN MOVING AWAY FROM STUCK BEHAVIOR

STUCK Behavior: Student cries and screams, "I want a turn!" when told to wait for a turn.

Adult: Says, "It is Jane's turn now; your turn next. When the red is gone (on the Time Timer®), it will be your turn."

STUCK Behavior: Student does not get off the swing at the park when the adult says it is time to go home.

Adult: Says, "When the red is gone, your turn on the swing is finished."

STUCK Behavior: Student begins to respond slowly.

Adult: While setting the Time Timer®, says, "Work for 5 more minutes. When the red is gone, you will be finished."

STUCK Behavior: Student perseverates or talks excessively.

Adult: While setting the Time Timer®, says, "When the red is gone, we will return to work."

9. STRATEGY: CHECK YOUR SCHEDULE

THE BASICS:

✔ Apply this strategy when students get STUCK in the middle of or between activities.

✔ Use a visual prompt (e.g., CHECK YOUR SCHEDULE card; see below and page 34).

✔ Communicate to students that the activity is ongoing and remind them what comes next.

✔ Place the schedule away from the activity so the student has to move to the schedule, thus providing a sensory break that may calm, organize, and/or alert the student (see STUCK Strategy 4).

MATERIALS:

- Student's visual schedule:

  - Object/picture/word schedule

  - Student agenda/assignment notebook

  - Adult appointment book

- CHECK YOUR SCHEDULE cards

check your schedule

- Student's individual schedule

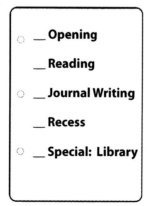

EXAMPLES OF USING THE STRATEGY TO SUPPORT STUDENTS IN MOVING AWAY FROM STUCK BEHAVIOR

STUCK Behavior: In the middle of Group Time, student says, "Is it time to go outside yet?"

Adult: Hands the student a CHECK YOUR SCHEDULE card. Points to symbols on the student's schedule with the student and says, "It is still Group Time now. You will go outside next. Let's get back to Group."

STUCK Behavior: Student stands in the middle of the room with a lost look on his face.

Adult: Hands the student a CHECK YOUR SCHEDULE card and waits to follow the student to the schedule.

Student: Puts the card in a preset pocket on the schedule, then looks to see what is next.

CHECK YOUR SCHEDULE

1. Copy page 34 on cardstock, laminate, and cut the cards apart.

2. Hand a card to the student when you use CHECK YOUR SCHEDULE.

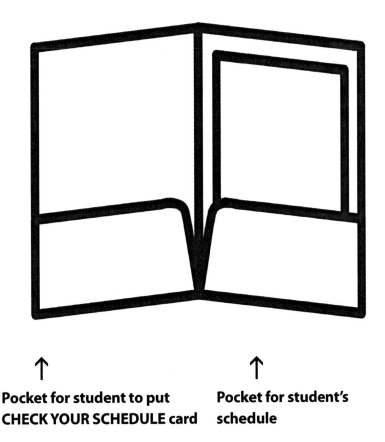

↑   ↑
Pocket for student to put   **Pocket for student's**
CHECK YOUR SCHEDULE card   **schedule**

check your schedule	check your schedule	check your schedule
check your schedule	check your schedule	check your schedule
check your schedule	check your schedule	check your schedule
check your schedule	check your schedule	check your schedule
check your schedule	check your schedule	check your schedule
check your schedule	check your schedule	check your schedule

10. STRATEGY: "DO ... THEN"

a.k.a. "NOW ... NEXT", "FIRST ... THEN," "Premack Principle," and "Grandma's Rule"

THE BASICS:

✔ Teach students that this means, "<u>Do</u> a less desirable activity, <u>then</u> you may do a more desirable activity."

✔ Utilize the opportunity to have students do a more desirable activity to reinforce doing a less desirable one.

✔ Structure motivating sequences of activities to ensure student effort and engagement. For example, begin and end the day with liked activities and intersperse familiar, tolerated activities with additional liked and some disliked activities throughout the day (Janzen, 2003).

✔ Realize this strategy involves more than alternating liked and disliked activities, since that may result in liked activities losing their power as reinforcers (Janzen, 2003). Be sure to include activities of varying levels of familiarity, difficulty, and preference to maintain the reinforcement value of preferred activities (Janzen, 2003).

MATERIALS:

- DO ... THEN board (see page 37)

- NOW ... NEXT board (see page 37)

EXAMPLES OF USING THE STRATEGY TO SUPPORT STUDENTS IN MOVING AWAY FROM STUCK BEHAVIOR

STUCK Behavior: Student starts to do NEXT step in a sequence rather than the NOW step.

Adult: Says, "Wash your hands NOW. NEXT you may eat," while pointing to a NOW ... NEXT board.

STUCK Behavior: Frustrated, student puts her head in her hands at the beginning of a writing assignment.

Adult: Says, "DO your sentences. THEN you may draw a picture," while pointing to a DO ... THEN board.

STUCK Behavior: Student attempts to climb out of the grocery cart while shopping with Dad.

Adult: Says, "Stay in the cart NOW. NEXT we will go to the playground."

REFERENCES:

Janzen, J. E. (2003). *Understanding the nature of autism: A guide to autism spectrum disorders* (2nd ed.). San Antonio, TX: Harcourt Assessment.

Premack, D. (1959). Toward empirical behavior laws: I. Positive reinforcement. *Psychological Review, 66,* 219-233.

DO ... THEN

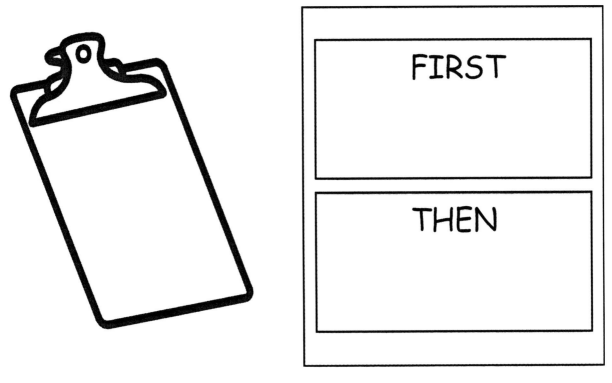

For a literate, middle school student, staff kept a stack of 8.5 X 11" pages on a full-sized clipboard. When the student got STUCK, the adult wrote the current activity in the "FIRST" box and the next activity in the "THEN" box. The staff saved the pages to track the frequency of the student's STUCK behavior as one measure of programming effects.

For younger students or nonreaders, use picture symbols on a small clipboard that can hang on a hook for easy access.

11. STRATEGY: TEMPT

THE BASICS:

✔ Hook the student by your active participation.

✔ Start, demonstrate, or change the activity.

✔ Give the student time to get to "yes;" that is, allow the student time to work through being STUCK and choose to engage in the activity.

✔ Teach the student how to get started or return to an activity by demonstrating the first (or the next) step.

✔ Attend to the student at the first sign of her beginning or returning to the activity without any comment about her nonparticipation.

✔ Make a mistake or do something unexpected to TEMPT a student to participate. Keep in mind this form of the TEMPT Strategy works for some students but may confuse or upset others who do not understand humor or the unexpected.

✔ Use animated intonation, gestures, and facial expressions. Be playful!

MATERIALS:

• Developmentally appropriate materials and activities

EXAMPLES OF USING THE STRATEGY TO SUPPORT STUDENTS IN MOVING AWAY FROM STUCK BEHAVIOR

STUCK Behavior: Student does not help put groceries away when asked.

Adult: Picks up a can and playfully puts it near its usual place in the cupboard. Play may include tapping the can on the shelf or moving it in the air to attract the student's attention.

STUCK Behavior: Student stops in the middle of a puzzle and wants to quit.

Adult: Picks up a puzzle piece, plays with it, and puts it near its proper place. Play may include tapping the piece on the table or moving it in the air to attract the student's attention.

STUCK Behavior: Student crawls under the rice table when asked to work with the other students.

Adult: Plays with the materials and interacts with students who are active at the rice table. The adult may verbalize sounds of play but does not interact with the student under the table.

12. STRATEGY: "THREE MORE"

THE BASICS:

✔ Recall the concept that being closer to the "finish line" increases motivation.

✔ Illustrate that the activity *will* end before long.

✔ Be mindful that the adult, not the student, determines what "THREE MORE" means (e.g., time, number of trials, number of math problems).

✔ Do **NOT** specify units (minutes, trials, pages, etc.). The vagueness of "THREE MORE" gives the adult the flexibility to use judgment to maintain the student's effort and end the activity contingent upon appropriate student behavior.

✔ Represent the student's renewed effort by removing chips from a "THREE MORE" box or making tally marks on a whiteboard as needed to keep the student motivated and engaged.

MATERIALS:

- To make a "THREE MORE" visual support, you will need:

    – Clipboard or plastic box

    – Poker chips or tokens

    – Hook-and-loop fasteners

EXAMPLES OF USING THE STRATEGY TO SUPPORT STUDENTS IN MOVING AWAY FROM STUCK BEHAVIOR

STUCK Behavior: With 10 more math problems to complete, student says, "I'm tired!"

Adult: Says, "THREE MORE and you are finished."

(Adult makes a tally mark at variable intervals, keeping the student engaged; for example, after two more problems, then after four more problems, then after the student completes all 10 problems.)

STUCK Behavior: Student puts her head on the table during a speech-language therapy session.

Adult: Says, "THREE MORE and you are finished."

(Adult removes chips from a "THREE MORE" box at variable intervals, keeping the student engaged; for example, after two more responses, then after five more responses, then after one more response. The adult or student may put the chips in the box through a slot cut in the top. Some students may enjoy shaking the box for a few seconds.)

13. STRATEGY: "SOON"

THE BASICS:

✔ Consider that the word "soon" provides for a gentler, less abrupt transition to the next activity.

✔ Use "SOON" as a "2-minute warning" to get the student ready for a transition or as an encouragement to keep the student working because the activity will end shortly.

✔ Avoid demands for immediate action, which may provoke a knee-jerk reaction of "NO."

✔ Communicate gentle support and respect for students' efforts and tell them the activity will end in a short time.

EXAMPLES OF USING THE STRATEGY TO SUPPORT STUDENTS IN MOVING AWAY FROM STUCK BEHAVIOR

STUCK Behavior: The student shows subtle, nonverbal signs of fatigue, frustration, and/or anxiety such as laying head on the table, sighing, fidgeting.

Adult: Says, "SOON you will be finished." Then, within a short time, the adult says, "The activity is finished."

STUCK Behavior: The student turns away from the activity.

Adult: Says, "SOON you will be finished." Then the adult directs the student back to the task and tells her that she is finished with the activity after working for a moment or two.

14. STRATEGY: CHANGE ADULT

THE BASICS:

✔ Change the adult interacting with the student while maintaining the same limits and expectations.

✔ Make sure that all adults are in sync and that they trust and support each other.

✔ Communicate to students that the system remains the same regardless of which adult is sitting next to them.

✔ Remember that a student may feel STUCK being with the same adult; changing the adult offers a bridge to getting unSTUCK.

✔ Keep in mind that students may feel they are wearing down one adult. Change the adult to communicate that all the adults support the system.

✔ Reach full understanding among the adults that this strategy is not about which adult is more skilled in working with students or more liked by the students but about the student getting unSTUCK.

✔ Make adult changes smoothly, nonverbally, and respectfully of everybody involved.

EXAMPLES OF USING THE STRATEGY TO SUPPORT STUDENTS IN MOVING AWAY FROM STUCK BEHAVIOR

STUCK Behavior: The student bangs his head against the table.

Adult: The adult working with the student first ensures the student's safety, then tries a few STUCK strategies. The adult then nonverbally signals to another adult in the room the need for CHANGE ADULT. The first adult moves away, and the second adult steps in with the same expectations.

STUCK Behavior: The student lies down on the floor in the hallway while walking back to the classroom from OT.

Adult: The adult says, "It's time to go back to class" and tries other STUCK strategies; for example, giving the student a weighted object to carry back to the classroom. Another adult walks by, and the first adult whispers, "Tell the student it's time to walk to class." Then, after exchanging a nod of understanding, the second adult says, "It's time to walk to class."

15. STRATEGY: "BE FINISHED"

THE BASICS:

✔ Allow the student to "BE FINISHED," contingent upon appropriate behavior.

✔ Remember that appropriate behavior may mean one on-task, desirable, or positive action, NOT necessarily completing the activity initially expected by the adult.

✔ State the appropriate behavior to be demonstrated, then say, "We can BE FINISHED."

EXAMPLES OF USING THE STRATEGY TO SUPPORT STUDENTS IN MOVING AWAY FROM STUCK BEHAVIOR

STUCK Behavior: A student who stayed on task and worked for a reasonable length of time calmly asks, "When can I go back to my classroom?"

Adult: Says, "You worked for 10 minutes. We can BE FINISHED now." (While this may reinforce the student asking to go back to the classroom, we see the student asking a question as self-advocacy and more desirable than running away or other acting-out behaviors.)

STUCK Behavior: A student who was STUCK and came back to being engaged in the task (not necessarily finishing the activity), sighs heavily.

Adult: Says, "You came back and did more work. We can BE FINISHED now."

References

Fisher, A. G., Murray, E. A., & Bundy, A. C. (1991). *Sensory integration: Theory and practice*. Philadelphia, PA: F. A. Davis Company.

Greene, R. W. (2005). *The explosive child: A new approach for understanding and parenting easily frustrated, chronically inflexible children*. New York, NY: HarperCollins.

Henriksen, K., & Kaup, M. L. (2009). Supportive learning environments for children with autism spectrum disorders. *Undergraduate Research Journal for the Human Sciences, 9*. Retrieved from http://www.kon.org/urc/urc_research_journal9.html

Janzen, J. E. (2003). *Understanding the nature of autism: A guide to autism spectrum disorders* (2nd ed.). San Antonio, TX: Harcourt Assessment.

Mayer-Johnson. (2008). *Boardmaker plus! v. 6*. [Computer software]. Solana Beach, CA: Author. (www.mayer-johnson.com)

Ory, N. (2007). *Working with people with challenging behaviors: A guide for maintaining positive relationships*. New Lennox, IL: High Tide Press.

Partington, J. (2010). *The assessment of basic language and learning skills – revised* (Vol. 3). Pleasant Hill, CA: Behavior Analysts.

Premack, D. (1959). Toward empirical behavior laws: I. Positive reinforcement. *Psychological Review, 66*, 219-233.

Savner, J. L., & Myles, B. S. (2000). *Making visual supports work in the home and community*. Shawnee Mission, KS: AAPC Publishing.

Schopler, E., Mesibov, G., & Hearsey, K. (1995). Structured teaching in the TEACCH system. In E. Schopler & G. Mesibov (Eds.), *Learning and cognition in autism* (pp. 243-268). New York, NY: Plenum Press.

Trott, M. C., Laurel, M. K., & Windeck, S. L. (1993). *SenseAbilities: Understanding sensory integration*. Tucson, AZ: Therapy Skill Builders.

Williams, M. S., & Shellenberg, S. (1996). *How does your engine run?: A leader's guide to the alert program for self-regulation*. Albuquerque, NM: Therapy Works.

Suggested Readings

Attwood, T. (2007). *The complete guide to asperger's syndrome.* London, UK: Jessica Kingsley.

Bernard-Opitz, V., & Häußler, A. (2011). *Visual support for children with autism spectrum disorders.* Shawnee Mission, KS: AAPC Publishing.

Biel, L., & Peske, N. (2005). *Raising a sensory smart child: The definitive handbook for helping your child with sensory integration issues.* New York, NY: Penguin Books.

Brewer, R., & Mueller, T. (2008). *Strategies at hand: Quick and handy strategies for working with students on the autism spectrum.* Shawnee Mission, KS: AAPC Publishing.

Brewer, R., & Mueller, T. (2010). *Strategies at hand: Quick and handy positive behavior strategies.* Shawnee Mission, KS: AAPC Publishing.

Buie, A. (2013). *Behavior mapping: A visual strategy for teaching appropriate behavior to individuals with autism spectrum and related disorders.* Shawnee Mission, KS: AAPC Publishing.

Buron, K. D., & Curtis, M. (2012). *The incredible 5-point scale* (2nd ed.). Shawnee Mission, KS: AAPC Publishing.

Fisher, A. G., Murray, E. A., & Bundy, A. C. (1991). *Sensory integration: Theory and practice.* Philadelphia, PA: F.A. Davis Company.

Fuge, G., & Berry, R. (2004). *Pathways to play: Combining sensory integration and integrated play.* Shawnee Mission, KS: AAPC Publishing.

Hodgdon, L. (2000). *Visual strategies for improving communication: Practical supports for home and school.* Troy, MI: QuirkRoberts Publishing.

Janney, R., & Snell, M. E. (2000). *Teacher's guides to inclusive practices: Behavioral support.* Baltimore, MD: Paul H. Brookes.

Kerstein, L. H. (2013). *A week of switching, shifting, and stretching: How to make my thinking more flexible.* Shawnee Mission, KS: AAPC Publishing.

Manasco, H. (2006). *The way to A: Empowering children with autism spectrum and other neurological disorders to monitor and replace aggression and tantrum behavior.* Shawnee Mission, KS: AAPC Publishing.

Maurice, C. (Ed.). (1996). *Behavioral intervention for young children with autism: A manual for parents and professionals*. Austin, TX: Pro-Ed.

McConnell, K. (2007). *Practical ideas that really work for students with autism spectrum disorders*. Austin, TX: Pro-Ed.

Myles, B. S., & Southwick, J. (2005). *Asperger syndrome and difficult moments: Practical solutions for tantrums, rage, and meltdown* (2nd ed.). Shawnee Mission, KS: AAPC Publishing.

Partington, J. (2010). *The assessment of basic language and learning skills revised* (Vol. 3). Pleasant Hill, CA: Behavior Analysts.

Rogers, S. J., & Dawson, G. (2010). *Early start Denver Model for young children with autism: Promoting language, learning, and engagement*. New York, NY: Guilford Press.

Savner, J. L., & Myles, B. S. (2000). *Making visual supports work in the home and community*. Shawnee Mission, KS: AAPC Publishing.

Wild, G. (2013). *Developing effective sensory diets: Seminar manual*. Franklin, TN: Summit Professional Education.

Williams, M. S., & Shellenberg, S. (1996). *How does your engine run?: A leader's guide to the alert program for self-regulation*. Albuquerque, NM: Therapy Works.

APPENDICES

APPENDIX A
Guiding Principles

Your EXPLANATION Guides Your INTERVENTION.

– Ross Greene

Plan for a student's WORST day.

It Takes a TEAM!

Be proactive!

Think antecedents, not consequences.

Proactive approaches lead to supportive practices.

Reactive approaches lead to punitive practices.

Behavior IS Communication.

When you see confusion, offer a peaceful, helping hand.

– Nathan Ory

Children do well if they can.

– Ross Greene

APPENDIX B
STUCK Strategies
(At-a-Glance)

STUCK STRATEGIES:
WHAT TO DO WHEN A STUDENT GETS STUCK

1. Be sure the activity is **DEVELOPMENTALLY APPROPRIATE & MEANINGFUL**

2. **COMMUNICATE YOUR EXPECTATION** that the student will start/finish the activity
Example: with your proximity to the student, body language, nonresponse to refusals

3. Use a **VISUAL SCHEDULE** and the words "**FINISHED, NOW, NEXT**"
Example: "___is finished. Now it is time for___. Next will be ___. Let's go to ___."

4. Offer a **SENSORY BREAK**, then return to the activity
Example: 10 jumps on a trampoline.

5. Offer **CHOICES** within the ongoing activity
Example: "Do you want to use red paint or yellow paint next? ...to walk with ___ or___?"

6. Say "**COME, DO, START**"
Example: "Come to the table. Do the animal puzzle. Start with this piece."

7. Give the student a **PROP** (object to hold), a **ROLE** (job to do), and a **RULE**
Example: "Please carry these books for me. We do math at the group table."

8. Use a **VISUAL REPRESENTATION OF TIME**
Example: "When the red is gone, your turn on the swing is finished."

9. **CHECK YOUR SCHEDULE**
Example: Hand the student a **CHECK YOUR SCHEDULE** card. Check that according to the schedule it is still time for the activity. Then <u>return</u> to the activity.

10. Use "**DO ... THEN**" (**NOW ... NEXT or 1ˢᵗ ... THEN**)
Example: "DO (the task at hand), THEN you may (a desired activity)." (with visual supports)

11. **TEMPT** the student by starting/demonstrating/changing up the activity

12. Use "**THREE MORE**"
Example: "Three more and you are finished." (with visual supports)

13. Say "**SOON**"
Example: "Soon you will be finished." Then finish the activity within a short time.

14. **CHANGE ADULT** interacting with the student while maintaining limits/expectations
Example: Waiting out a tantrum – Change adult after 5-10 minutes without explanation.

15. Let the student "**BE FINISHED**"
Example: Hand the student a **CHECK YOUR SCHEDULE card**, check the schedule, then go on to the next activity.

APPENDIX C
STUCK Strategies Worksheet

Use the worksheet as a tool to plan which STUCK Strategies to try in activities during which students get STUCK. Take data in the far-right column to evaluate the effectiveness of the plan.

STUCK STRATEGIES WORKSHEET

Student's Name: **Date:**

When (activity or time)	the student (behavior)	try these STUCK Strategies:			DATA		

Related

The Incredible 5-Point Scale:

The Significantly Improved and Expanded Second Edition; Assisting students in understanding social interactions and controlling their emotional responses

by Kari Dunn Buron and Mitzi Curtis

Using the same practical and user-friendly format as the first edition, Buron and Curtis let readers benefit from work done with the scales over the past 10 years, now considered "classics" in homes and classrooms across the country and abroad. Includes new scales specifically designed for young children and those with more classic presentations of autism, including expanded use of the Anxiety Curve. Another welcome addition is a list of goals and objectives related to incorporating scales in students' IEPs. Also, a free CD includes blank scales, small portable scales and worksheets for easy duplication. As in their other writings, the authors emphasize the importance self-management and self-regulation, two evidence-based practices.

ISBN 9781937473075 | Code 9936A | Price: $19.95

A Week of Switching, Shifting, and Stretching

How to Make My Thinking More Flexible

by Lauren H. Kerstein, LCSW

This picture book assists children on the autism spectrum, and any child for that matter, in examining their black-and-white thinking in order to begin to think more flexibly – rainbow thinking. Using repeated rhymes and illustrations, the child begins to recognize that the more flexible his thinking is, the better he is able to cope with the challenges that life inevitably brings, ultimately, leading to fewer tantrums and meltdowns.

ISBN 9781937473891 | Code 9108 | Price: $17.95

Behavior Mapping

A Visual Strategy for Teaching Appropriate Behavior to Individuals With Autism Spectrum and Related Disorders

by Amy Buie, MEd, BCBA, LBA

Playing to the visual strengths of students with autism spectrum and related disorders and their need for structure and consistency, Behavior Mapping helps children make good choices with regard to their behavior by visually showing them available options and the consequences for each action they choose at any given time. Due to its visual nature, this strategy, whether paired with written and/or oral directions, is effective for a range of students, regardless of age and ability level. Built upon evidence-based practices, their are three major types of Behavior Maps – Consequence Maps, Language Maps, and Problem-Solving Maps, each serving a different purpose aligned with common areas of difficulty for students with social-cognitive challenges.

ISBN 9781937473822 | Code 9107 | Price: $19.95

Visual Support for Children With Autism Spectrum Disorders

Materials for Visual Learners

by Vera Bernard-Opitz, PhD, and Anne Häußler, PhD

With hundreds of colorful illustrations and step-by-step directions, this book lays the foundation for how to structure teaching environments, as well as offers countless examples of activities for students, ranging from basic skills, to reading and math, to social behavior. The authors have combined their years of experience working with individuals on the autism spectrum to bring teachers and other professionals practical ideas and teaching methods for offering visual supports to students with ASD and other visual learners.

ISBN 9781934575826 | Code 9065 | Price: $34.95

To order, please visit www.aapcpublishing.net

AAPC Resources

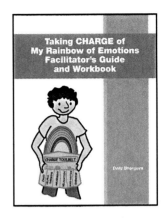

Sensory Issues and High-Functioning Autism Spectrum and Related Disorders

Practical Solutions for Making Sense of the World

by Brenda Smith Myles, PhD, Kelly Mahler, MS, OTR/L, and Lisa Robbins, PhD; Foreword by Winnie Dunn, PhD

Using the same practical and easy-to-read format as the first edition, this newly expanded book explains how many children with high-functioning ASD relate to the world through their senses. The book reviews sensory processing terminology and how the sensory systems impact behavior. An expanded discussion of assessment tools is followed by a comprehensive chapter on evidence-based interventions. Finally, a new chapter looks at meeting a student's sensory needs throughout the day and across environments using simple and easy-to-use forms and checklists.

ISBN 9781937473778 | Code 9907A | Price: $21.95

Social Rules for Kids

The Top 100 Social Rules Kids Need to Succeed

by Sue Diamond, MA, CCC

Social Rules for Kids helps open the door of communication between parent and child by addressing 100 social rules for home, school and the community. Written directly to the student, these clear rules cover topics such as body language, manners and feelings. Reminders of appropriate social rules at the end of each page are combined into a complete list for easy reference.

ISBN 9781934575840 | Code 9067 | Price: $19.95

Totally Chill: My Complete Guide to Staying Cool

A Stress Management Workbook for Kids With Social, Emotional, or Sensory Sensitivities

by Christopher Lynch, PhD

When parenting, teaching and working with children who have social, emotional and/or sensory sensitivities, we often put the emphasis on learning new skills. Countless hours are spent working on social skills, fine- and gross-motor skills, language skills and academic skills, but stress management skills are often left unaddressed. This is unfortunate, as stress can create a multitude of challenges for learning and daily living. In other words, it can create barriers to the very things we are trying to teach. Besides, it can cause distress, which can lead to meltdowns and behavioral outbursts. In short, it is crucial that children learn and develop skills to help them to manage their stress as independently as possible. This book s a stress management workbook that is meant to be read, completed and used as much as possible by children themselves.

ISBN 9781937473044 | Code 9079 | Price: $21.95

Taking CHARGE of My Rainbow of Emotions

Facilitator's Guide and Workbook

by Dolly Bhargava

Identifying, expressing, and dealing with their emotions in a socially acceptable way poses challenges for many children with autism spectrum and related disorders. Starting with checklists for assessing one's emotions, this innovative resource goes on to provide caregivers with a framework for giving students the tools they need to become effective emotional managers. Using the visual of a tool belt, strategies are grouped into the following categories: Chat Tools, Help Thinking Tools, Amusement Tools, Relaxation Tools, Good Routine Tools, and Exercise Tools – all tools proven helpful for individuals with social-emotional challenges. Lots of forms and visuals make this a practical and ready-to-use guide.

ISBN 9781937473938 | Code 9113 | Price: $25.95

To order, please visit www.aapcpublishing.net

PUBLISHING

P.O. Box 23173
Shawnee Mission, Kansas 66283-0173
www.aapcpublishing.net

CPSIA information can be obtained
at www.ICGtesting.com
Printed in the USA
LVOW09s1542111217
558736LV00015B/19/P

9 781937 473990